I0455366

Training IVY

How to Become the First Practicing Female

African-American Oral and Maxillofacial Surgeon

in both the Commonwealth of Pennsylvania and

the Commonwealth of Virginia

by Dr. Julia L. Jackson

Chapter 1

Where should I begin? Well, immediately, the first person that comes to mind is my wonderful mother. Her motivation and inspiration are the main ingredients to my dedication. You see, my father was an electrical engineer and patented inventor, he has since passed, but I believe his ability to problem solve and think creatively helped mold me into the scientist that I am today. As an adolescent I was a handful to say the least, awards, honors, suspensions, disciplinary actions and Class President of the Freshmen Class, a true mix bag of adolescent mischief, perseverance and self-determination. I finished ninth grade from Friends Select School a small private school located in center city

Philadelphia. A curriculum based on Quakerism. A way of teaching and instruction that I had become very accustom to since pre-kindergarten grade at age 5. A soft spoken passive environment. This education was nurturing but stale and traditional. By seven, eighth and ninth grade, my pre-teen hormones and adolescent behavior caused major conflict with the peaceful, non-confrontational Quaker values. I was considered "hyperactive" and "boisterous" they practically called me "out of control" . Unfortunately this required my mother to have more than her fair share of parent teacher conferences. Although those initial struggles in school were self-defeating, the obstacles and challenges now appear self-induced. I was aware of my internal conflict. Once I came to understand that my behavior sets the tone for my environment. I came to understand that my actions could come to good use. I realized I could use my actions, and disposition to have a quite or peacefully atmosphere or I could be intensely disruptive in my environment. Understanding having the power over my action and untimely leading to power over my surroundings was a lot to conceptualize as a young adult. My growing and development were multifaceted. Physically growing, emotionally growing, and developmentally growing simultaneously. Frequently outside influences can be disruptive. Fortunately for me internal conflicts were my biggest challenge. Self-control, learning to remain quiet, actually siting still for long periods of time these were the most difficult. I am glad that I never gave up. I am glad to have had steadfast support. At all times I believed in my goals. Part of my story is the fact that I identify as African American or simply put I am a person of color. As a person of color attending two different predominantly Caucasian Elementary school I was always one of the few people of color in my grade let alone my entire school. So at the end of ninth grade after not being asked to return for tenth grade due to disruptive behavior, I asked my parents if I could

attend a school with more students "of color".
My parents and I decided I would attend one of the very elite three public magnet schools in Philadelphia.

Central High school was coed and was the largest of the three. The Philadelphia High School for Girls was my mother's alma mator. George Washington Carver High School of Engineering and Science was the one I chose. The school was located downtown on my mother's way to work and in the direction of my younger brother s school, Friends Select School. Each morning my mother would take my brother and I to school, this was very important time to gather our thoughts and discuss our goals for the day. Carver High School of Engineering and Science was an environment that included adolescents from the neighborhood and other neighborhoods in Philadelphia. This was a very unique experience for me. I was able to learn coping skills. This was an opportunity to continue to build myself determination and self-resilience. I instinctually followed my mothers sound advice I was very quiet in high school, it was as if in this environment I had become the soft spoken non confrontational peaceful person. Quakerism had made a great and positive influence on me. These are the characteristics I try to emulate on a daily basis to this day. In high school I changed and grew and developed. I had friendships and acquaintances outside of the school.   High School would not be my last exposure to a culture shock, nor was it was my first. The shock itself was the jolt of feeling different, feeling the difference and in this case feeling uneasy.   Since I started a new school in tenth grade all the high school cliques were formed so I was the new girl who "talked like a white girl. "I tried not to let these things get me down. Instead I began to understand other people, as an outsider, I became more of an introverted personality with much self-reflection. While steadfastly narrowing my focus on my goals, which at that time was graduating from high school. I was on the track team, and I very much enjoyed my drafting class in high school. I learned very quickly home work was important. I attentively sat in the front of the class. I diligently would prepare for my tests. I was on the honor roll and senior year I earned straight A' s. I was granted an opportunity to have a senior year of high school externship. My project was an internship with the department of public health. I worked in a Philadelphia Department of public health Free Sexually Transmitted Disease Clinic, it was located on Broad Street in South Philadelphia. I would spook to my peers about the importance of having safe and protected sex. Frequently teenagers would come to the clinic for check ups. I ran a young adults sexual education after school program. I would dispense reading materials and condoms. As a senior in High School, my final presentation was a Power Point presentation. I spoke in depth about sexually transmitted diseases such as Syphilis, Gonorrhea, Chlamydia, HIV, Herpes and genital warts (HPV). I displayed very large graphic photos for effect. I delivered important facts and education. I very much enjoyed teaching and informing my classmates.

When I graduated from Carver it was 1997, and I had already participated on several college tour trips. The college tour trip is an essential part of how children formed their understanding of higher education. These trips assist high schoolers in forming their understanding of what it means to attend college and live away from home on a college campus. As an adolescent very rarely do you get to see a college campus. There are many mysteries, such as where is the cafeteria, how are the sleeping arrangements, what does the scenery and the landscaping look like; but college tour trips and specifically tour trips that are engineered by parents, where you and mom go directly to the school, are extremely helpful for expanding one' s mind and seeing the colleges up close.

My mother took myself and several of my friends to visit Fordham University, to visit Hofstra University, and to visit several other universities including Ursinus in Pennsylvania and the Barnard College in New York. My mother was very active in social groups as we were growing up. The Alpha Kappa Alpha sorority incorporated, The Links and my mother was a Jack and Jill of America mother. As a member of Jack and Jill of America, in the summer months a Historically Black College (HBCs) bus tour was organized for the regional groups. I attended the bus tour with my friends and a few parent chaperons. We visited the college campuses of HBCs which included Morgan University, Spelman University and Hampton University.

As the story goes I was allotted great opportunities to see and visit several college campuses prior to making the absolutely best decision to choose the college I ultimately attended and graduated from. The most remarkable, that held a lasting impact was "Pre Frosh weekend" . Pre frosh means pre freshmen weekend. This was intended for graduating seniors from high schools from around the country who had high academic scholastics. These interested students were invited to attend Wesleyan University Prefrosh Weekend. This weekend ultimately made all the difference. Wesleyan University in Middletown, Connecticut. The entire weekend was to introduce the potential students to Wesleyan University campus, student body and faculty. We toured the Campus including the dorms, the student union center, and the theater and arts buildings. We visited the science libraries, the gym and sports fields. The entire campus was sprawling and beautiful. Although it was not very big the campus was bordered by the residential neighborhood of Middletown Connecticut.

I distinctly remember the Saturday evening of the Pre Frosh weekend. The university had planned a music concert for the entertainment of the visiting students and the entire campus body. The visiting students were matched up with a "Wes- Connects" who was a current Wesleyan student. I stayed with her for the entire weekend. Together my Wes Connect and I walked across campus from her dorm towards the cafeteria. We walked through the grassy knolls of Foss Hill, going toward the cafeteria where the concert was being held. The cafeteria was a doomed shaped structure the doom was all glass and the walls were full windows from floor to ceiling as well. Although I walked up to the door from the outside, the inside entry was an elevated foyer the structure was two stories tall, the entry was on the second level. This structure was surrounded by a vast wooded area, except for the entry. I recall walking down into the cafeteria. Traveling down the long curved stairwell to the bottom level where there was a stage that was set up with microphone stands and very large mega big speakers. That evening Groove Theory sang and entertained the potential Wesleyan newcomers. They rocked the house. The concert was awesome. The music filled the room, the people began to dance and my sensation of feeling free and able to be me overwhelmed me. That evening I grew into who I have become today. The powerful feeling of self-enlightenment and rejuvenation overwhelmed me. It was truly a moment of self- awareness.

CHAPTER 2

Wesleyan University- Middletown, Connecticut

It was August 1997 and my mom and dad and younger brother Thomas were dropping me off at college. We had packed both cars with all my vital belongings from Philadelphia and we were in the parking lot saying goodbye. I was very, very nervous. Wesleyan. It was a time of new beginnings.

My energy was ignited like fire! My mind was racing. Was I going to be able to graduate? I was so scared to disappoint my parents. I was so nervous and worried and thinking to myself, "Oh my! Is this really where I am supposed to be? How is this going to work out? What am I going to learn? What am I going to do? Who am I going to meet? Can I meet the man of my dreams? Am I going to find a romantic love? What is this "college thing" all about?" I remember standing in the parking lot thinking to myself as my father was unloading my belongings into my new dorm on Foss Hill. I remember distinctly saying, "Mom, I am so worried. I am not sure if I am going to be able to graduate." She told me, "Julia, you have gotten this far. You know that there are things that are going to be a challenge but there is going to be obstacles that you are going to be able to get over, under, or around." She said, "Julia, there is no doubt in my mind that there will be a day in 2001 that you will be graduating happily from this university and I will be even more happy than you. So please get yourself together and get yourself on your way." I said, "Thank you mom," because she always seemed to have a way to say exactly what I needed to hear to get me back on my steps in the right direction to fulfill and satisfy all of my goals.

The summer before the first semester of college which began in September I was in a summer enrichment program. This was an Advanced Science Masters/ PhD program. This program was held on the Wesleyan campus but it was off campus housing. This was an important summer program for a selected group of students that was held before the regular semester began. This program was called "3000 by 2000" led by Dr. James Donady PhD. This elite academic program was an opportunity for me to get a prior understanding on the sciences that are required for an MD or a PhD program. At that time, I was much focused. I have always been dedicated to education and understanding that at an early age, it is important to focus on your goals and focus on the things that you want to accomplish. You have to put blinders on to narrow your perspective to get your mind attuned to what it is that you have set forward to accomplish. I found it curtail not to become distracted by nay Sayers. I believe that it is important to not let people who have not accomplished your goals try to direct you away from your goals. During the program I was able to meet other premed students who I liked very much, they were people of color from other places, NYC, CA NJ, MA, and they were smart and welcoming. Especially since we were all new. This was an invaluable experience. In addition the older college student showed us the ropes and made lasting friendships. They helped us coordinate our academic courses and reminded us to have fun. By this time in my life I was starting to realize when you do good, it makes other people happy. I realized not to be persuaded to do things simply because it's not usually done that way. As a college freshmen I was realizing exactly who I wanted to be. Most importantly I redirected my rebellion to become an unstoppable positive force. I wanted to accomplish goals that most people did not. So for instance Wesleyan is one of the few schools where students pick their own curriculum there was no standard curriculum. There were major requirements based on credit hours. The 3000 X 2000 program was an opportunity for me to be mentored. My mentor and I strategically constructed my course curriculum. I completed all of my Pre-Med Prerequisites in addition to majoring in Psychology. Early in my academic career, I was informed that you needed to major in Biology or Chemistry to become a doctor and I wanted to prove that wrong from the beginning. I was determined to major in something other than Biology or Chemistry. Psychology peaked my interest and became my designated major. I was able to take an architecture class and a sculpture class, both of these allowed me to expand my conceptual abilities and manual dexterity. I was able to take dance courses and message class. I took African American studies including the study of Tupac Shakur the lyricis and poet. During my third year of Wesleyan I went on a semester abroad. I lived Baja California

Sur Mexico, in La Paz. I was a Coastal Ecology student, studying in Bahia Magdalena. The research groups would break up into 5 groups of four students. We all worked together. There were several teachers, there were people that prepared our food and local fishermen who were our boat guides, we all became a very big happy family. Most of the staff spoke Spanish so I was able to fufill my Spanish requirement for graduating. Each of us had research projects based on sustainable development. Our purpose was to determine whether or not the resources were being depleted. We each studied a component to the ecosystem. The foundation layer to the ecosystem is the ground surface. In this case I was studying the floor of the bay where there was sand and sediment. I would collect samples and count the microscopic benthic invertebrates in each sample. I compared the amount found in the different areas of the shore line.

My friends studied the blue crabs, dolphins, pelicans and fish. Each studied how the ecosystem was effected and the impacted on sustainable development. The community of Bahia was that of a fishermen town. There was a fish canning Plant in town and the fish where caught in great quantities daily. My particular research project included gathering small samples of sediment in different locations of

Bahia Magdalena Bay. In these different areas I collected sediment samples which contained small benthic invertebrates. The research focused on the quantities of those fundamental organisms to the food chain. I compared locations and quantities, this comparison would lead to the conclusion of weather the food chain was plentiful or depleting. Weather sustainable development was taking place or were the natural recourses being abused either due to Human pollution of the bay or Human consumption by over fishing. If the microorganisms were depleting then an imbalance of the ecosystem would take place. If the fishermen' s boats were the cause of pollution to the bay than the microorganisms would be decreased which would lead to inability for the small crustaceans to feed which would affect the small fish which would affect the birds which would affect larger mammals which would ultimately lead to decreased natural resources. My research concluded that there was a sustainable development. I was able to prove that the resources Bahia Magdalena were not showing signs of potential problems of pollution or microorganism depletion.

Although throughout high school and early college research has been a place of comfort. At an early age and grade I was told that I was displaying a slow development the teachers reported to my mother that I was behind in my reading level. Between 6th and 7th grade I changed schools. For only one year, I attended a school for children with learning challenges. My class consisted of 12 boys and one teacher. Studies have subsequently shown boys are more likely to have dyslexia and most of my classmates were dyslexic, many of them were diagnosed with Attention Deficit Disorder, and or Hyperactivity Disorder. I turned out not to have a learning disorder at all. I was however very hyper and perhaps easily distracted. The way that we were being taught during the semester abroad program was interactive and enter related. We worked together. This was a very rewarding academic environment for me. This was the first time for` me to be in a learning environment where we the students learned together and worked together. We used tangible learning processes and hands on understanding.   We gathered each other' s samples and helped calculated each other' s data. All of our materials and slides were shared. I was very happy to participate in such a meaningful way. I was grateful to be a part of their research as well as I appreciated their contributions to my research. My colleagues during this spectacular experience and adventure were studying other species. We counted the pelicans, and caught the crabs, and photographed the whales, we searched for dolphins. Because we worked so closely with the local residents we were also afforded the opportunity to work on our Spanish. Each of us became fluent Spanish speakers to some degree. I completed my pre-med biology requirements including life science. I had opportunities to make new friends I had a wonderful and a fabulous semester abroad experience. As a Coastal Ecology student we would sit on the sandy beaches and make a campfires, and we would tell stories and discuss sustainable development practices. We began to teach each other and learn from each other as well. We began to understand how humans and nature interacted with each other. We studied how the food chains and the complex ecosystems related. We slept in thatched roof cabins on the school grounds. We held classes in the class room and on the beach. Early in the mornings before sun rise we would meet the boat guides by the motor boat docking area. We were required to wear our life jackets and we would pile into the motor boats. We would head out on the water to a pelican feeding area to count the birds until sunrise when they would begin to fly off for the start of their day. We would wade in the water in the evenings and we would see the small plankton swimming on the surface of the water. They would glow in the dark. The little organisms were a mesmerizing array of bright colours in the water. They appeared to have electricity running through their transparent exoskeleton or a chemical reaction that allowed them to appear to be illuminating in the water. It was unique and vividly imprinted in my mind. We ate great food, lots of fish, lots of crabs, lots of healthy vegetables, and tomatoes. In November 2000, for Thanksgiving dinner celebration, as a group we travelled by minivan down town to purchase food from the local market. The feast was a pulp Erie of traditional Mexican and American thanksgiving dishes. I ate everything that was delicious which was everything and it was a very beautiful cultural experience. Occasionally in town I would feel the culture shock, a feeling I can recall. This circumstance of culture shock was due to the differences in traditions and cultural customs. The money was different, the language was different, and the customs were different. The most obvious difference was how much differently the people looked than my Philadelphia neighbours and people from the states. The men were a lot shorter in Mexico, the women were equally as petite, the children were very beautiful with long straight dark hair and dark eyes, and the parades were fabulous. The music and dancing were spectacular events. The people of the town noticed me as well. They saw a recognition that my skin, sun kissed and golden brown was very similar to theirs. Unlike my follow research colleagues and friends I was the only African American student. I was noticed and embraced by the locals. Although the local residents were shy they would frequently felt comfortable enough to approach me while speaking in Spanish. As if this life altering, cultural, scientific, learning experience could not get any better it did. The last two weeks of the semester we were encouraged to go together as a group to explore other areas of Mexico. This was an opportunity for me to go to Cabo San Lucas, the most Southern point of Baja California Sur peninsula. This was an opportunity like no other. Wesleyan University gave me experiences of being able to strategize and learn and eventually graduate. My mother was right as she always is. I graduated In May 2001 with a Bachelors of Arts in Psychology. In addition I completed my pre-med prerequisites including chemistry, biology, biology life science, organic chemistry, statistics, and physics. I was accepted into Wesleyan University Master' s degree program in psychology. It was a fifth year program where I would earn a Master' s in one additional year making me a viable candidate for a PHD program in Psychology or a very competitive candidate for medical school with a focus in psychiatry. Either way a fifth year at Wesleyan sounded like a great idea to me. I absolutely loved my entire college life. I believe this nurturing educational experience only polished my true appreciation for education. The majority of my growth and development has occurred while I have been attending school. After graduating from high school in 1997 I attended formal school training and hospital surgical residency for an additional 14 years.

CHAPTER 3

I digressed, I took a short trip. Well, it turned out being a lot longer than I expected, but I took a trip in 2001 on a train ride from Philadelphia to California. My purpose was to go to California because I have never been there before. I intended to visit family and to visit a possible new job opportunity. This would be my first job. It was a private dental lab that I found in California. I looked into this is because I wanted to explore all possible job options. I also took a standardized test called the "DAT." The Dental Administration Test was a conceptual test with sections in both mathematics and science. It was a dental school entrance exam. Similarly to the MCAT for medical school, and the LSAT for Law school. I studied and took the DAT. I had taken previous standardized tests but I have never been very good at taking test. At that point in my life I knew I wanted to be called Doctor and help improve the lives of others. I wanted to do something more hands on than being a family practitioner. My father' s words of wisdom really came in to play at this time. All of those many cherished moments working with him in our in home laboratory. Valuing the passion and feeling of accomplishment I shared with my dad when we work with our hands. I certainly had refined my childhood curiosity. I had sharpened my manual dexterity skills while taking courses in high school and now college. My father was first to suggest I attend dental school. At that time I was not sure if I needed to be a dentist to do what I wanted to do which was work with my hands. So I looked into this dental lab tech facility in California the summer I graduated from Wesleyan, while the news of dental school acceptance was still pending. That summer I was also holding an acceptance to Wesleyan University School of Psychology. I was rostered to be getting a master' s degree in the five year program. I knew that I had just taken the DAT to prepare for going to dental school and I would receive the results over the next few weeks. I was either going to be a dentist or a psychologist. That summer, I decided to go to California. I traveled across the country by train. It was an overnight train for at least a week. My mother was very nervous about this voyage. But she had taught me well, I did not sit next to any strangers, I kept my self safe. I caught the train on a Sunday and during the course of several days, I travel all across the country. The strain stoped occasionally to let people on but I did not get off of the train until we reached Los Angeles. We passed different areas that I had only heard of before including, Ohio, Indiana, Missouri, and Albuquerque. I remember the conductor announcing when we crossed the Mississippi River. Once I arrived in Los Angeles, California, I rented a car and I drove to gardenia and visit my cousins. I stayed with my cousins for a several days. I left Gardenia and drove to up to Carmel Valley and I spent four months in Carmel Valley in Monterey, California with a good friend of mine from Wesleyan. My friend was in the process of moving so I was there to help her pack her entire house of belongings. During my visit I set up a job interview at a very big and productive dental lab in Northern California. The lab was a distribution center where custom made dentures and prostheses were made, crowns and dental bridges were fabricated in this facility as well. This lab was near Monterey in the area of Carmel Valley. They gave me a tour of the facility and interviewed me. They explained that they were dental lab technician most of the employees were artist, many of them had attended tech schools. They asked me about my work experience which I had none, they asked me about my schooling they understood that I was college educated. I conveyed that I had just graduated from one of the most prestigious "little" Ivy League universities in the country. I informed them that I had a BA in Psychology and had completed my Pre-Med prerequisites. This interview was awkward they told me that I was overqualified to work as a dental lab technician. I told them I wanted to work with the paints and the ceramics and I wanted to use the instruments and they told me that they believe that I was overqualified and that this was not the right position for me. I thanked them and I left. I ended up spending the whole summer in California. I traveled to San Francisco, visiting Berkley University. I visited Hollywood and Disney World. I laid on the beaches of San Cruz and enjoyed the sunshine. Since my costal ecology studies in college, when I travel to a new beach I collect sand and a water samples. I have since collected from over 15 beaches. That summer I took an airplane back from California to Philadelphia. When I arrived home I received call from the dental lab inviting back to work full time. I also received a letter in the mail stating my acceptance to Temple University School of Dentistry.

CHAPTER 4

In 2001, I began my first year of Temple University School of Dentistry located in Philadelphia, Pennsylvania. Being a Philly girl and being at home from Connecticut was truly a wonderful, wonderful opportunity. It was just my luck that I got an opportunity to go to Dental School in Philadelphia. When I finished college in Connecticut, I was exploring the opportunity of UConn as my first choice. The University of Connecticut School of dentistry was located about an hour away from Wesleyan University. It was a dental school that I did not visit but was well aware of because they specifically recruited graduates from Wesleyans 3000 by 2000 program. 3X2 students   were top students interested in a medical or dental profession. Temple University Dental School is in my hometown and was a school I was more familiar with. My mother frequently attended University of Pennsylvania Dental School for all of her teeth cleaning and routine dental care. So when I found out that I was accepted to Temple University School of Dentistry I was very, very happy and proud of myself to be chosen to be one of the new students for the Class of 2001. During the first few weeks and months of dental school, while I was taking the basic sciences such as Organic Chemistry, Chemistry, Biology, Anatomy, Pharmacology and Physiology including Histology which is the study of the cells and human DNA, I realized that all of these hard sciences were very complicated and very overwhelming. Although I excelled in my Oral Pathology and Basic Pathology courses some of the other sciences were more challenging than I had expected. I was very depressed during this time. I carried feelings of oppression and depression during the first two years of dental school. It was not until the third year of dental school that my hopes began to rise. I realized we were going to be working in clinical settings, doing more craft work and eventually treating patients in the clinical setting. Finally I could begin working my hands.

I was nominated and voted Vice President of my class in my first year of dental school and I was elected Secretary of the Oral and Maxillofacial Surgery Honor Society in my third year. I very much enjoy holding leadership positions. Those positions I held to their highest regard although I felt significant discrimination from some of the senior faculty and teachers during my training as a dental student at Temple University. I hold no grudge because I have certainly risen to the top. I am very comfortable in my status but the discrimination that I felt when I was there did not make it any easier. It only made it harder and more frustrating. Yet much much more rewarding and satisfying now that my career and professional goals have been reach. I have successfully become the first and only African-American female Oral and Maxillofacial Surgeon practicing in both the Commonwealth of Pennsylvania and Commonwealth of Virginia in 2016. I know the discrimination encompassed the seed but I certainly did not let it spoil the fruit. Once I took out my first tooth in the third year of dental school, I was absolutely 100% sure that Oral and Maxillofacial Surgery would be the specialty that I would pursue. You may or may not be aware that there are seven established fields of dentistry.

The fields include general dentistry which I think of as a base and foundation of dentistry. General dentistry is th e restoration and the preservation of teeth after they have been deemed decayed or unhealthy and or requiring repair. Second on the tier the pyramid of dentistry fields, I would consider would be periodontics, which is the study of the gingiva and how the teeth function in the gingival soft tissue which covers and protects the bone which is the hard tissue. Periodontics is the study of the soft tissue around the bone and its relation to the tooth structure and tooth stability. Periodontists remove teeth. They place implants. They do gingival surgeries and they specifically are helpful with keeping the areas clean and are known for deep cleanings and scaling of the tooth surfaces.

The third tier working our way up, I would suggest would be endodontics which is the study of the anatomy in the tooth itself. In the tooth there is a nerve supply and that nerve can be deadened so that the tooth no longer has vitality and no longer has any feeling or elicits a pain response. The specific study of the removal of the nerve in the tooth is endodontics.

The fourth tier would be the movement of teeth. To move teeth, you need to apply braces and orthodontics is the specialty that masters in tooth movement. Teeth must be moved through bone this will allow the soft tissue to follow. It is important to predict soft tissue changes once the teeth have been mobilized. Orthodontics

Next and close to the top, I would say would be pediatric dentistry which is specializing in dentistry for children. All of the previous tiers would be applied for diagnosis and treatment for children. Children require all the same care in dentistry as adults but frequently managing the child' s behavior is what makes this specialty unique. Children require treatment such as cleanings, moving teeth, repairing teeth, and restoring of teeth if necessary doing root canals and extractions are performed on children. These procedures may require putting the child to sleep for the treatment to be performed in a safe manner.

The next tier would be what I would refer to as prosthodontics which is the false replacement of teeth. If a tooth is determined not to be healthy or it cannot be fixed, or is in the wrong location, is not in function or susceptible to infection that tooth should be removed. If the tooth is removed then it needs to be replaced and the specialty that focuses on the replacement of teeth that are removable is a prosthodontics.

Last but certainly not least, the pinnacle of dentistry is Oral and Maxillofacial Surgery. We as surgeons specialize in diagnosis and treatments of the head and neck from the cranium to the clavicles. If a patient was found to have head and neck pathology or a broken bone or a facial laceration, a particular anatomical deformity or a dental deformity resulting in a malocclusion we treat full scope of oral and maxillofacial surgery patients. We treat the way the teeth come together. We treat head and neck cosmetics including frown lines, between the eyes or a wrinkle around the corner of the eye. We also preform cosmetic face lifts. Oral and Maxillofacial surgery is the specialty that focuses on the head and neck reconstruction. Including bone graft and implant placement and reconstruction of the facial skeleton and cranium. Our ultimate goal is to restore function while achieving optimal facial esthetics. Oral and maxillofacial surgery is the ultimate pinnacle of dentistry.

When I was in fourth year of dental school, I was honored for my academic achievement and high academic standing. I had completed multiple extra-curricular hours and requirements and I was granted an opportunity to participate in a self-directed oral surgery externship. I chose to work with the Temple University Hospital department of Oral and Maxillofacial surgery. I shadowed the oral surgery residents and observe the surgical attendings in the operating room cases. Oral surgery is a specialty that requires hospital exposure, frequently cases are treated in the hospital setting. Generally oral surgery residency programs are hospital-based programs. Oral and maxillofacial surgery residency training can be independent from the associated Dental School and university. Oral and Maxillofacial surgery can be solely taught in a hospital setting. Temple University Oral Surgery residency program is separate from the dental school, unlike with Howard University oral surgery residency program where the dental school and the hospital work intricately with the purpose of having a well-balanced curriculum. When there is a teaching relationship and an opportunity to take advance courses in the dental school a camaraderie is established between the residents and the dental students. My Temple dental undergrad curriculum was very separate to have an externship with the Temple University Department of Oral and Maxillofacial Surgery was a very special circumstance as a third year dental student. The residency program utilized several local hospitals, I visited the smallest one, a clinical/ teaching hospital called Episcopal Hospital that was off campus. This was a clinic with 4 operatorys, three out of the four were used for intra venous sedation procedures. During my rotation, twice a week for six weeks, I was able to take out teeth with the residents and help the residents treat sedated patients.

During the rotations I volunteered to attend 5 am rounds. I went to the OR early in the mornings and late, late at night. I would observe surgeries. I observed awesome pathology cases and severe trauma reconstruction cases as well. I recall the removal of a superglotic ranula. This soft tissue mass cased significant elevation of the floor of the mouth. They removed the ranula from the floor of the mouth. I observed the surgical repair of facial bone fractures, gunshot wounds to the face, sever laceration repair and elective procedures like orthognathic surgeries. I was intrigued, this was my first exposure to surgery and operating room protocol. I observed surgeries for hours and hours and hours. Sometimes the time was spent contouring metal bone plates to adapt to the bone to facilitate the mending and repair of a broken jaw or repairing and mending orbital floor fractures by bending and molding the plate that they slipped beneath the globe so that the globe has sound support and the vision is corrected. These were just a few of the many procedures that oral and maxillofacial surgeons routinely preform. By fourth year of dental school I had made the decision that I was officially interested in pursuing oral and maxillofacial surgery residency. This was a highlight of my fourth year. I finished on a positive note with all of my requirements, taking out more teeth than just about anyone in my class and perfecting my skill at how to take out teeth efficiently and relatively painless. I also looked forward to pursuing oral surgery residency. I was apprehensive because of the amount of years involved with further training. I knew being a general dentist was not an option because general dentistry did not interest me at all. A passion and desire began to grow in me. I was determined to become an Oral and

Maxillofacial surgeon. I realized the surgical programs were four years with certification or six years programs for certification and a medical degree. At the time just finishing an intense four year undergraduate dental curriculum I was interested in a one year internship. Although the programs are four and six years there are preliminary positions referred to as internship year. These positions are for students interested in oral surgery residency positioned but since the residency programs are very competitive and highly selective some programs have one or two internship position spots available. This was the type of position I was seeking.

So after graduation in 2005, I pursued an internship at the University of Pennsylvania in Philadelphia. I specifically sought out this particular program because it would allow me to stay in Philadelphia but most importantly, I had previous opportunities to work in the operating room with the UPENN surgical residents and faculty surgical attendings before during my senior externships. While at PENN I saw cases there that truly intrigued me. They were moving the mandible forward, which is the bottom jaw, forward to help repair or treat sleep apnea. A patient came in for consultation. He was a gentleman had sleep studies and be evaluated to determine that he was apneic during sleep.   Apneic means he was not breathing or exchanging oxygen sufficiently to oxygenate the brain. If you do not breathe while you are sleeping, it can cause a lot of imbalances and dysfunctions to your system. It can cause hypertension.   It can cause hypoxia which is inability to have oxygen. It can cause problems when you do wake up, because truly you are not sleeping peacefully if you cannot breathe while you are sleeping. Somnolence is not being able to sleep. Somnolence can lead to being sleepy when you are supposed to be awake because you did not sleep well; so sleep apnea is serious and causes many different detrimental health effects.

University of Pennsylvania is a research based program. They were studying and comparing the effects of surgical treatment options. Sleep Apnea is something that can be surgically treated by repositioning the lower jaw forward. There are other ways of solving the problem as well. Surgical repositioning has the highest success rate and outcome. Because of the complexity of the anatomy involved with sleep apnea the evaluation of the elasticity of the soft tissues of the oral pharynx is required. This can be examined utilizing the Muller technique and a complete ear, nose and throat exam. Static and dynamic movement evaluation is critical as well the elasticity of the muscles in the posterior oral pharynx become very loose with age, which can contribute to sleep apnea. UPENN oral surgery program was trying to find out whether or not the best treatment of sleep apnea included surgical management. Beking at University of Pennsylvania exposed me to a research based residency program. I really like it and I wanted to stay for the one year internship position. I shadowed the attendings and attended grand rounds. But low and behold they did not chose me for the position. My time spent a UPENN turned out to be to my benefit only. The exposure allow for me to observe and be a part of a surgical training program. The experiences and learning that I took away was very valuable. Although when I found out I was not selected for the internship position I was crushed. My disappointment was short lived. I was able offered a great opportunity to interview for an internship position in The Oral Surgery Department in Brooklyn, New York at the Brooklyn Hospital Center. I ended up staying for a second year fellowship in oral and maxillofacial surgery. I lived in Brooklyn from 2005 to 2008.

By now in my academic life I had graduated from dental school with a special interest in specializing in Oral and maxillofacial surgery. I was not married with no children and I was 27. I was living in Philadelphia in a two bed room apartment in a home attached to the home my mother grew up in in north Philadelphia. This house is the primary residence for my uncle Louis. I was delighted to move to The Brooklyn Hospital Center. This was also my first time having a paid position. I was given a stipend and my rent was paid. The housing was provided for me because I asked if there was ant housing available. I was very fortunate to stay in a large studio apartment in a New York high rise building. I stayed on the 10th floor and on the second floor was a bridge that attached to the hospital. It was perfect!! In 2006, myself and another female were the interns at Brooklyn

Hospital Center. She was honored with the opportunity to no longer be an intern but to move up in to the next status of being a first year resident at Brooklyn Hospital Center. When we found this out, it was during the time of a program called "Match." Match is a residency program lotto all over the country. It is a particular day all over the country where the dental students get matched with dental residency programs. This is a lotto because there are very few residency program positions and a select few of oral surgery four year or six year residency applicants. Most of the programs have 1-3 residents in each year so a total of 12 residents per year for a four year program. There are less than 50 oral surgery residency programs over the country. In 2006 it was a requirement that dentists needed to have one year of residency before they could go into private practice. Now, I had had my one year of residency from 2005 to 2006, so this was my second year, but nonetheless when my co intern Ann was offered the opportunity to stay at Brooklyn Hospital Center as a first year resident, she turned it down and she told the program and the program director that she did not want to be part of the program at all and she left, leaving a vacancy in the internship position and leaving a vacancy in the first year position. I was not offered either position. Match took place and the program was matched up with a first year resident. They then offered me to be an intern a second year and I took it. From 2006 to 2007 I was at Brooklyn Hospital Center as a second year as an oral and maxillofacial surgery surgical resident intern, and that year I applied to at least 25 different oral surgery four year residency programs. I very much enjoyed those two years. I lived in "the big apple" . I lived in the very convenient hospital apartments. They provided this housing to me for a very reasonable discounted rate. I had a spectacular view of the New York City skyline including the Brooklyn Bridge. There was a large very tall sky-scraping high rise, on the second floor there was a tunnel or bridge that connected to the hospital. This was the very best for me for early morning rounds and late evening emergency trauma call. I was very fortunate that I could go upstairs to my room or I could come down to the hospital very quickly and efficiently. I would go to the Emergency Room; take care of patients; go walk through the bridge and get right back to my home. It was really a perfect opportunity, the rent was not too high and I was able to save money and I was able to enjoy my work, and I studied and I learned a lot and it was a wonderful time in my life at Brooklyn Hospital Center.

In 2007, I travelled to California again and this time I went specifically to King Drew Hospital in Los Angeles. I visited the Oral Surgery Program with Dr. Leathers who was the director of the program. I was informed that the program was merging with harbour view hospital. I met many of the residents and I met the chief resident and I saw how their program operated. It was good to see other people of color as oral surgery residents. Both Temple and PENN were all white males. I was impressed and wanted to participate. I thoroughly was anticipating working in California as a resident. While in California I visited UCLA medical center I shadowed the oral surgery residents for the day in the clinic. I travelled to southern California and I visited an oral surgery program in Fresno California. I visited several programs all over the county. When I got returned to New York I visited Woodhull Hospital in Flatbush, Montefiore Medical center in the Bronx and I visited Harlem Oral Surgery program as well. At each visit I interviewed with the director of the program, I met with the residents and I shared my interest and experiences. I provided each program director a copy of my curriculum vieate. When I found out through Match in 2007 that I had matched to Howard University Hospital in Washington D.C., I was very shocked and surprised. I had interviewed with the director of

Howard University Hospitals program the year before in 2006, I did not expect an acceptance a year later. I did not know the program at Howard had voted to choose me. I was not initially happy because I did not necessarily want to attend Howard, a Historically Black University. Most of the programs were 12 to 18 residents of all white males and a handful of Asian males. The program directors and attendings were white males. The hospital staff and doctors were predominantly white throughout my travels to different residency programs. Although that was the case I was very apprehensive to attend Howard University Hospital. My mind wonders back to the isolated feeling I had at Carver High School among people of color. It is very uncomfortable at first, yet I believe now it was a very good answer to my prayers but I did not know that at the time. At the time, I believed I was going to go to California and so I called the California program to find out why they did not pick me and they told me that their program was shutting down due to the merger of the two hospitals. They did not want to choose me knowing that the program was not on solid ground. They thought it would be better for me to get into another program for sure, and then they would have given me the option to transfer if I wanted. So after understanding why (and I am very glad I know why because I thought they did not like me

after they did not choose me but it was not that)
after understanding why, I did choose to stay
with the Howard University Hospital Four year
Oral and maxillofacial surgery residency program.
I also bought my first home in 2007 I was 29
years old. It was a studio condominium within
walking distance of university campus as well as
walking distance to Howard University Hospital. I
started my life on 2nd and V Street North West.
My first home purchased allowed me to use a
doctors mortgage loan, where my debt to
income was not factored in. Instead they looked
at my average future earning potential. I was able
to use some of the money I saved during my
internship years in New York for the down

payment and good faith estimate. The unit that I purchased in 2007 is still mine today and it is certainly a rewarding investment property. I attended Howard University for four years from 2007-2011.

CHAPTER 5

My father used to say "listen to your counsel" he referred to this statement for two reasons he believed I would benefit from checking with my advisors when making important decisions and because my mother would always be my first counsel being that she was a lawyer prior to becoming a Judge. My counsel in this case was Dr. Leathers the program director from King / Drew medical center. He explained to me, when you are going to invest the next four years in a residency program he suggested I also invest in real estate. He insisted that I buy a home and that I plan not to rent for four years but instead purchase a new home or condominium. I agreed. I made a personal goal that I would strongly consider being a first time home owner when the time came to start a four year program. This self-proclamation required preparation.

I walked into the bank. I discussed with a counter representative my interest in a new home purchase, she suggested I speak with a mortgage loan specialist. With a loan officer I sat face to face to discuss how to get a home mortgage, what the requirements where, and the application process. I ended up opened a Wells Fargo bank account. But I walked away with invaluable information and educated mortgage vocabulary. I took what I had learned about the process and I called a second bank, I was able to speak intelligently to the mortgage specialist at SunTrust. Within 2 months I closed on my first home purchase. It was a success. I scouted this new construction out on the internet while living in Brooklyn, New York. My mother was very concerned that I was buying my first house without seeing it! I explained to her that it was a new construction in Washington D.C. within walking distance of Howard University Hospital. So together, she and I went to Washington to meet the real estate agent who was selling the newly constructed units. We each took the train her from Philly and I from New York and we met in Washington D.C. We took a cab to the property address. Sure enough, the three story low rise condominium was in the process of being constructed. This building was on the corner of second and Vest streets, the condominium consisted of a total of three buildings. The second building referred to as Gage school was a renovated old school converted into condominium units. The units eventually finished with beautiful large windows and high ceilings. The home I purchased was in the new construction, on the first floor above a basement unit. My mother and I each wearing a hard hat stood on the reinforced concreate floor and discussed the ultimate floor plan with the sales agent. The unit was a work in progress and it was beautiful to me. I am sure my mother was thinking that this was a great risk. I was thinking it was a very good start. We had entered the unit by walking up the front steps from the outside but there were no walls or doors. We entered the area that was designated as mine, this was before the walls were constructed and the drywall had been placed so it was very open and empty but nonetheless, we evaluated the premises, pointed out designated areas for the bath room tub, laundry area and kitchen sink. We visualized my studio apartment. This area of 500 square feet would be my very own little piece of the world. While my mother approved, somewhat, I knew that this was going to work out.

By August 2007, I had moved to D.C. to begin my surgical residency program. I stayed in a temporary housing arrangement where I was renting a room month to month. I lived in small room in a house and waited for my home to be completed for me to move in. The property was not completed until November. I moved in shortly thereafter, no more than four months and it was absolutely beautiful. Granite countertops, stainless steel appliances, hardwood floors, indoor laundry, and bay windows. It was very spectacularly beautiful. The walls were freshly painted, the doors and windows were trimmed. It is a very beautiful little place. I was a perfect, private, healthy space for me to study. I was so proud of myself for making great decisions by following sound advice. This was such a good start and it was a wonderful place for me to grow and develop.

Oral and maxillofacial surgery is a very intricate and detailed practice of science and surgery as well as a practice of medicine and surgical skill. It is a practice of dentistry, and it is a profession that can be technically challenging. For me it is extremely gratifying. I truly am in love with my craft and my field, my specialty, my surgical skill, my ability to see problems and fix them, and notice if things can be better. I thrive to make sure that someone is more comfortable or more at ease. I am committed daily to help patients. Oral and maxillofacial surgery covers such a variety of topics. There is a broad spectrum of very specific topics. There are ten subjects which include Anesthesiology and Pain Control, Dentoalveolar Surgery, Facial Trauma, Temporal Mandibular Joint evaluation and treatment, Head and Neck Pathology, Facial Cosmetics, Medical Assessment and Management of the Surgical Patient, Orthognathic/ Cleft / OSA Surgery and lastly the bread and butter of most oral surgery private practice offices is Dental Implants and oral reconstruction. Each of these ten areas of study are complex and complicated. These ten topics are interdisciplinary.

Oral and maxillofacial surgery is the only specialty, medical doctors or dentistry specialty, who sedate patients in the private office setting. Oral Surgeons also utilize operating. I routinely sedate patients in my safe and properly equipped office space. My active anesthesia license permits the administration of sedation medication in the state of Virginia.

Oral and maxillofacial surgery is a specialty that repairs cleft lip. It is a specialty that does facial reconstruction. It is a specialty that repairs broken bones to the face. During residency I conducted a research study to determine the probability of determining whether a female patient evaluated in the emergency room would be able to be diagnosed to have sustained injuries as a result of domestic violence based on the pattern of her facial injuries and fracture patterns. Frequently victims of domestic violence do not report the assault. I was looking to find patterns in facial bone fractures in victims of domestic violence. My purpose was to expand domestic violence awareness in teaching hospitals. I intended to show identifiable patterns of facial bone fractures that are frequently sustained as a result of domestic violence. I was able to gather enough data to prove nasal bone fractures and orbital floor fractures were frequently found to be related to injuries resulting from domestic violence.

Oral and maxillofacial surgery is a specialty who are first responders for trauma patients. We manage trauma patients of all ages including a small child who may have has hurt his front teeth while playing. We communicate to parents, how we can replace these teeth and stabilize these teeth, and help to encourage this person to keep their teeth. Oral and maxillofacial surgery helps patients replace teeth with dental implants, dental reconstruction, removing wisdom teeth that are impacted in the bone, removing pathology that has eroded bone in the face, mouth or jaw. Oral and maxillofacial surgery is a broad-spectrum with many subjects and specifics. It is an absolutely beautiful, beautiful opportunity for someone to expand their mind, to utilize their hands, to master science, to figure out anatomy, to look for details of beauty, to look for details of cosmetic or aesthetically pleasing symmetry. Oral and maxillofacial surgery is a field of study for any young creative mind to explore and learn and treat and care for people. If not using your hands clinically, then research and understand is an option. Oral and maxillofacial surgery is an academic subject of interest which is always in need of more academic facility and academic research. Most importantly, oral and maxillofacial surgery is a small group of specialist. Our expertise and ablity to surgically treat patients is endless and universal. I can help patients that do not speak my English. I can take out a tooth on any person successfully with the appropriate equipment and the appropriate lighting. If I can see it, I can take it out. So, I say this to say as an oral and maxillofacial surgeon I believe there are maybe 2,000 oral surgeons in the country. If there are 2000 oral surgeons in United States of America across the country, 500 of them maybe women. Of the 500 women, 100 of the women are women of color; and of the 100 women of color oral surgeons, 20 of those women are African-American; and of the 20 Africa-American oral surgeons that are women in United States of America, I am the only one located in the Commonwealth of Virginia and the Commonwealth of Pennsylvania.

Chapter 6

I believe to appropriately understand who I am you will need to understand my bloodline. I was born on Tuesday May 30th, at the University of Pennsylvania Hospital in the morning. This was a scheduled procedure because I was in a breech position. Even to this day I am ready to jump out feet first. My Mom used to say it was the potato salad from the Memorial Day picnic that instigated her labor pains. I am my mother and fathers first born and only daughter. I am the oldest grandchild and only female first cousin out of four. This makes me very much loved and cherished. My brother is four and ½ years younger than I am. My family is very close. My dad has two sisters and my mom has two brothers. Both of my parents and aunts and uncles were born and raised in Philadelphia. My father Thomas H. Jackson III, Tom the bomb as he was known to go by, married my mother Frederica A. Massiah on August 10, 1974. When they met, my mother was a recent graduate of University of Pennsylvania Law School and my father was working as an electrical engineer. They met at a Kappa Alpha Psi fraternity party. My mother told me she was dating a member of the Black Panther party when she met my father. Coincidently when my father introduced my mother to his parents for the first time, my mom and my fathers, father, recognized each other from both working at Philadelphia' s 30th street

United States Post Office. My father's father, Thomas H Jackson was a postal worker for many decades. My mother sorted mail at the post office for one summer in law school. Upon my father introducing my mother to his parents she was welcomed into the Jackson Family immediately. My father also felt a mutual respect while establishing a relationship with my mother's father. My Father expressed to me that because both men were engineers they understood each other and shared common experiences. My father had a great admiration for his father in law. My grandfather Fredrick Massiah was certainly a man to admire with an intriguing story of his own.

Chapter 7

My grandfather Frederick McDonald Massiah was born in Barbados, West Indies on December 12, 1886. He immigrated to the United States in 1909, where he started as a laborer, working during the day and studying architecture at night. My grandfather Massiah studied at the Pennsylvania School of the Fine Arts and earned a degree in Civil Engineering at what is now Drexel University located in Philadelphia. By the early 1920s, he established his own business. My grandfather Massiah was one of the first successful African-American contracting engineers in the United States; establishing a business during a period when it was nearly impossible for minorities to obtain financing, insurance, and acceptance in the trade unions. At the time, he became a leader in the use of reinforced concrete in building construction, starting with the Walnut Park Plaza Apartments in 1927. His method of using reinforcements in concrete pre-dated the existence of widespread building codes in the 1920s. By using a combination of concrete and steel acting as a unit, rebar in concrete, high tensile qualities of steel allow concrete to stretch and twist with greater yield strength than concrete that is not reinforced, while helping prevent cracks in the structures from changes of temperature and shrinkage.

My grandfather Fredrick Massiah's many accomplishments included the elliptical dome of the Ascension of Our Lord Church (the first structure of its kind in the U.S.), the William Donner X-Ray laboratory at the University of Pennsylvania, and the Sewage Disposal Plant in Trenton, N.J.

My grandfather Massiah was awarded the William E. Harmon Foundation Medal for Engineering in recognition of outstanding beam and girder work, and it was cited as a model by the Philadelphia city engineers to the University of Pennsylvania's engineering program in the Towne Scientific School. Having established his firm' s reputation, he went on to have a 45 year career, receiving numerous private and government contracts. Including the Capehart Housing Project at Fort Meade, MD, and the Morton Housing Development. My grandfather was a member of the Phi Beta Sigma Fraternity, the Philadelphia Chamber of Commerce, the Masonic Order, and the National Association for the Advancement of Colored People. My grandfather became a U.S. citizen on April 29, 1931. He married my grandmother Edith Lamarre in 1950.

Chapter 8

Edith Lamarre Massiah was born in Port-au-Prince, Haiti on June 18, 1918. She was educated in Haiti at the Ecole Normal and was awarded an academic scholarship to study at Ohio State University in 1946. She went on to earn a bachelor's degree in education from St. Joseph's University and a master's in social work from Temple University. Between 1965 and 1975 she taught French at the Baldwin School in Bryn Mawr, PA. My grandmother also worked as a social worker in Philadelphia for the Department of Public Welfare, the North Central Philadelphia Mental Health and Mental Retardation Community Center, and Catholic Services. Her and my grandfather married in

1950. They had one daughter, my mother Frederica and two sons, Allen and Louis. My grandmother Edith Massiah is my name sake. I hold her madian name of Lamarre. My grand mother was raised speaking French, she spoke with a French accent and she spoke French to me as a child. She was very fair complection with soft brown hair. I was 13y the majority if the family this was a years old when she passed away and my brother was 8. She was affectional called Mere Mere by most of the family this was short for Gra Mere which is French for grandmother. Mere Mere died on May 5, 1991. My grandfather Massiah died on July 7, 1975, I was born three years later.

Chapter 9

Frederica Massiah-Jackson

Most people call her "Your Honor", most people call her Mrs. Jackson, some people call her Freddie, but I call her mom.

My mother is a truly unique individual. She is a little bit short. She is certainly direct and very specific. She has a contagious smile and internal strength. My mother is very conservative. My mother is exactly what a judge should be. She thoroughly fits the position of her profession. She is stoic, she is hardworking and she is determined.

My mother is a Philadelphia Court of Common Pleas Judge. She was President Judge from November 2000 to November 2006. She graduated from the Philadelphia High School for Girls in three years at the age of 16. She also graduated from the very prestigious all womens catholic college, Chestnut Hill College in three years and the University of Pennsylvania Law School in 1974 at the age of 23. My mother and my father were married in 1974 and I was born when she was 28. Following law school, my mom clerked for Pennsylvania Supreme Court Justice Robert N.C. Nix, Jr.; he later became Chief Justice of the Court. She joined the Philadelphia firm Blank Rome Comisky & McCauley in 1976 and stayed with the firm until her election to the bench in 1983. My brother was born in 1983 as well. I was five years old.

On July 31, 1997, my mother was nominated to be a Judge of the United States Court District for the Eastern District of Pennsylvania. She was nominated by President Bill Clinton. I graduated from high school that year as well. My mom practiced corporate and civil litigation with the law firm of Blank Rome before advancing to the bench. My mom was a lecturer at the Wharton School of the University of Pennsylvania from 1992 to 2002; she also taught Legal Studies and Business Law. During her years as President

Judge from 2001 to 2006, she was the First Judicial District (FJD) administer justice with a $110 million overall budget and 2500 employees and 130 judges.

My mother, Judge Massiah-Jackson, is an effective leader in the Philadelphia courts. She held an innovative management role and facileatated advances in technology. Access to Justice was the hallmark of the FJD during those first years as my mother enhanced the publics perception of judges and the organization. Among the many projects, my mother the President Judge Emeritus coordinated court employee appreciation events, increased the pay rates for court-appointed counsel fees, signed a Mitigation Protocol for representation in the death penalty cases, opened a first judicial district information center, expanded our judicial education initiatives, and implemented programs to promote race and gender fairness within our courtrooms.

In 2011, Philadelphia's Mural Arts Program partnered with the university companies to include my mom on a mural entitled "The Faces That Shape Us". My mother Judge Massiah-Jackson received the 2010 NAACP Cecil B. Moore Award, and in 2007 my mom's portrait was presented to the courts and has been hung in the Ceremonial Courtroom of City Hall. In 2006, my mom was chosen by the Pennsylvania Commission for Women as one of the 50 women of color role models profiled in the book "Voices" . In 2005, she co-hosted Philadelphia's first Urban Courts Conference and she sits on the board of Center for Literacy and Eagleville Hospital, and is a member of the Forum of Executive Women. My mom is a member and past president of the Delaware Valley Pennsylvania Chapter of The Links Incorporated, and my mom is a member of Alpha Kappa Alpha sorority; as am I a legacy member. My mom, has received numerous awards and recognitions of service. She is a phenomenal woman.

Chapter 10

Let us not forget who brushed my hair, who bathed me, who put lotion on my body, who fed me, and who kept me warm during most of my toddler times. My grandmother, Joan B. Jackson, took good care of myself and my brother for many years and most of our early years. My grandmother today is 95 years old and she has been learning new things daily. Living the life in Sarasota, Florida, soaking up the sun and enjoying the company of other seniors in her assisted living facility, which I visited several times a year. She is comfort and stable and happy. My grandmother raised myself, my brother, my father and my two aunts. My grandmother is a great grandmother to my brother' s first child. She is certainly waiting for me to have a great grand for her as well. Joan B. Jackson, born in Little Rock Arkansas United States of America. In her home town there is a street named after her family name, Guydon Way. She was one of 20 children. Her mother was the elementary school teacher for the town at the time. My grandmother was a seamstress, dressmaker and tailor. My grandmother is a very good cook and homemaker. She certainly knew how to run a tight ship and keep me healthy, well-nourished and clean. My grandmother was my daycare during the day as my mother worked diligently in the Courts of Common Pleas. My father an Electrical Engineer, was delighted that his mother would have the opportunity to take care of me and my brother daily. My grandmother and my grandfather were married for 57 years. Thomas Holmes Jackson, Sr. is my grandfather's father. My grandfather, Thomas Holmes Jackson II, or Junior as they refer to him was born in Virginia. Thomas Holmes Jackson III was my father, and Thomas Holmes Jackson IV is my brother, and Thomas Holmes Jackson V, is my nephew and god son. There is a long life of legacy and pedigree. My family is the skeleton to my every move. Today, 2016, I am 37 years old. I am married to a wonderful and supportive man. We live happily in Washington, D.C. I am an oral and maxillofacial surgeon. I have mastered the full scope of maxillofacial surgery. On a daily and consistent basis, I help others with their surgical needs. As an Oral and Maxillofacial surgeon, I care for patients who are referred to me from their general dentist, and some who have sought me out for my specialty. Some days we have good days, and some days we have challenges. But each day, I am thankful for the blessings that God has bestowed upon myself and my family. Each day, I look to the Lord to say thank you for health and happiness and prosperity. Each day, I look to the Lord for my lineage, where I have come from, what it took to get me where I am, what does the Lord have in store for me for the future. At this ripe moment in my marriage, my husband and I are childless. We plan to start a family any day now. "Do I want a child? Do I need a child? Can I help raise a child?" Again, those questions circulate in my mind as they have before; questions of doubt, nervousness and worry that are conquered by my steadfast eagerness to learn and change and grow. I believe I will be a good parent. I will continue to strive to be an excellent wife. I know in my heart I will be a loving mother. Let us see what is next.

The Beginning

www.ingramcontent.com/pod-product-compliance
Lightning Source LLC
Chambersburg PA
CBHW020539290526
45786CB00002B/962